T0119452

the kitchen witch's
spell book

the kitchen witch's
spell book

spells, recipes, and rituals for a happy home

CERRIDWEN GREENLEAF

CICO BOOKS
LONDON NEW YORK

Published in 2021 by CICO Books
An imprint of Ryland Peters & Small Ltd
20–21 Jockey's Fields
London WC1R 4BW
341 E 116th St
New York, NY 10029

www.rylandpeters.com

10 9 8 7 6 5 4 3 2

A CIP catalog record for this book is available from the Library of
Congress and the British Library.

ISBN: 978-1-80065-040-4

Printed in China

Designer: Paul Stradling
Design concept: Emily Breen
Illustrator: Emma Garner

Commissioning editor: Kristine Pidkameny
Editor: Jennifer Jahn
Art director: Sally Powell
Production manager: Gordana Simakovic
Publishing manager: Penny Craig
Publisher: Cindy Richards

Contents

introduction
The Charmed Life

No matter how humble, kitchens are where we gather together. The very stuff of life takes place in this room—cooking, sharing meals, and talking about our lives. What can be more sacred than this? Nothing. For pagans, far more than meals are prepared in this space. All manner of concoctions and cures are created here. Herbs are ground up, blends are brewed, essential oils are bottled, healing teas are steeped, tinctures are carefully measured—to name but a few of the duties of the kitchen witch.

The kitchen of a witch is truly a thing to behold—a sacred space where good health, prosperity, and love can be conjured. The kitchen is truly the heart of the home, imbued with positive energy. Magic and spellwork are about expansion—expanding your horizons, enriching your mind and spirit, and celebrating the real riches of well-being and contentment. Every witch walks the spiritual path with practical feet, navigating the modern world aided by ancient wisdom, handed down generation after generation. When you begin to access this special kind of knowledge, you join a lineage of folks who are more in tune with the natural world around us—our Mother Earth, the moon and the stars, herbs and plants, animal allies. All these are nature's gifts and you will use them in the sanctity of your kitchen. As soon as you approach your magic consciously, you will see that you have the power to choose abundance. Then you can move on to the truest kind of prosperity, which has nothing to do with material gains, but involves sharing blessings with loved ones and your community. It is focused on creating meaning and happy memories.

Magic resides inside of us; we create it with our thoughts and actions. It is our deepest power and we are all born with it. The goal of ritual is to bring about needed change. It is how we make things better for ourselves, for our friends and loved ones, and for our community and our world.

a kitchen witch's toolkit

Your tools are instilled with your energy, storing power and magnifying the strength of your ritual work. Additional tools at your disposal are less tangible than knives, cauldrons, herbs, and wands; these are your breath, visualization, your intuition, and ability to focus your thoughts and emotions. Your intention purifies all these additional skills in your arsenal. As you walk the path of a sacred life, know that everything you do can be a vessel to carry enchantment. With this special mix of positive and practical magic, kitchen witchery can be your means to bring much good to the world.

Broom

This magical tool was born centuries ago from the practical magic of sweeping the ritual area clean before casting a spell. With focus and intention, you can dispel negative influences and bad spirits from the area and prepare a space for ritual work. In bygone days, pagan marriages and Beltane trysts took place with a leap over the broom, an old-fashioned tradition of handfasting, the classic witch wedding. Over the centuries, this rich history began to capture the imagination as the archetypal symbol of witches.

Your broom is an essential tool for energy management. Obtain a handmade broom from a craft fair or your favorite metaphysical five-and-dime. This should not be a machine-made plastic one from the supermarket, although I did get a long cinnamon-infused rush broom from Trader Joe's that I use in my witch's kitchen. A broom made of wood and woven of natural straw will be imbued with the inherent energies of those organic materials.

✳
BROOM ETIQUETTE

This is very important—do not use your ritual broom for housecleaning. Like me, you may well view every inch of your home as sacred space, but you will need to keep your regular housekeeping implements separate from those you use for your magical workings. Think of it as a separation of church and state, if you will. It pretty much is!

In general, it is not advisable to use tools such as your ritual knife to debone a chicken, for example, as this risks a confusing blending of mundane and magical energies. If you treat your ritual tools with the utmost respect, they will serve you very well. Over time, they will become inculcated with magic through exclusive use in your ritual workings. The Wiccan tradition holds brooms in high regard, and some witches have an impressive collection of brooms, each one named to distinguish their roles as "familiars," or kindred spirits. Kitchen witches often have the most extensive bevy of brooms of anyone.

Crafting Your Own Purification Broom

....

To purify your space with as much of your own personal energy as possible, a broom you have crafted by hand is best. You don't have to wait until you are holding a circle or even performing spellcraft—you can purify after a squabble with a loved one, to rid yourself of a bout of the blues, or any upset you need to sweep right out of your home. Many a kitchen witch begins the day with this simple ritual of a clean sweep to freshen surroundings and to make room for good energy in your life. Of course, this cleaning is not intended to make your house spotless; it is a symbolic act that is effective in maintaining your home as a personal sanctuary.

You can make your own purification broom from straw bound together and attached to a fallen tree branch, or you can add some mojo to a store-bought broom. Wrap copper wire around the bottom of your broom handle and also use it to bind straw to a sturdy stick or branch for the DIY kind. Venus-ruled copper lends an aura of beauty and keeps negativity at bay. You can attach crystals to the handle with glue to boost your broom's power. Recommended crystals for space clearing and purification are as follows:

* Amber for good cheer
* Blue lace agate for tranquility and a peaceful home
* Coral for wellbeing
* Jet absorbs bad energy
* Onyx is a stone of protection
* Petrified wood for security
* Tiger's eye will protect you from energy-draining situations or people
* Turquoise creates calm and relaxation

Cauldron

Here we have a true essential for kitchen witchery! The cauldron represents the goddess; its round basin is symbolic of the womb from which we all came. Ideally made of cast iron or another durable metal that heats uniformly, the cauldron can hold fire and represents rebirth, the phoenix rising from the ashes of the past. Usually, cauldrons stand on three legs for practicality, stability, and mobility. You can place one on your kitchen altar if there is room or on the floor to the left of the altar.

In spring, this sacred basin can be used to hold earth or water and, in the winter season, it should hold fire—candle flames or sweet-smoked incense, which signifies the rebirth of the sun to come at the end of the coldest season. You can also be playful with the form the cauldron takes and use a rain-filled urn or a flower-filled fountain. Summer's cauldron can be a beautiful cup; at harvest-time, use a pumpkin or another hollowed-out gourd. You can play with the vessel concept in your own ceremonies and be imaginative—get really creative.

A classic cast-iron cauldron is very useful for mixing your herbs and essential oils—just make sure to clean it thoroughly after each use so as not to mix energies inadvertently. You can scry with a cauldron full of water to foresee the future by reading images on the surface of the water, as well as use this magical vessel for burning papers upon which you have written spells, incantations, and magical intentions. In doing this, you are sending your wishes to the gods and goddesses through the flames, the element of Fire.

Chalice

The chalice—another vessel symbolizing the feminine, the Goddess and fertility—is a goblet dedicated specially for use on your altar. Holding both physical fluid and waters of our emotional body, it is connected to the element of Water. Place your carefully chosen chalice on the left side of your altar with all other representations of the energy of the female and the Goddess. A grail is also a chalice. Legend tells that the Holy Grail brought life back to the decaying kingdom of Camelot and restored King Arthur and his people to health, giving rise to the rebirth of England itself. On your altar, your chalice can hold water, mead, wine, juice, or anything that has been blessed. It can contain holy water for consecrations and blessing rites. At the end of many ritual ceremonies and sabbats, it is customary to toast the deities with a hearty ale, cider, or wine and thank them for being present. After the circle has been opened, you can pour the contents of your chalice into the ground outdoors as an offering to the benevolent entities.

Magic Bottles

Spell bottles, or magic bottles, have been around since the 1600s and were often filled with hair, nails, blood, and other kinds of ephemera. Now, they are used to empower us and adorn our sacred spaces. Though their popularity has waned since the Elizabethan age when they were called "witch bottles," they are still used for a variety of intentions, and your magical kitchen can display many a spell bottle. You can also customize your own spell-in-a-bottle with crystal stoppers and you should let your imagination run wild as to the usage and positive purposes with which you can fill your vessels: put one in your garden to keep your plants healthy, one in the bedroom to bring love and happiness, and a spell bottle on the living room mantel to protect your home. Spell bottles are used for protection primarily, but you can also put symbols of your dreams and desires in them—a rose for romance, cinnamon for the spice of life, and rosemary for remembrance.

SPELL BOTTLE SECRETS

To ensure that your kitchen is peaceful, secure, and grounded in "good vibrations," gather a teaspoon of clean, dry soil from outside your home and put it into a bottle with smoky quartz crystal, brown jasper, or any dark, earthen-colored semiprecious stone. Place the bottle in a potted herb on your windowsill and think about the sanctity of your space every time you water your plant. As your plant grows and thrives, so will the tranquility of your space.

A bottle with a rosebud or rose petal, rose essential oil, and rose quartz next to your bedside will help with love. For six days, rub oil from the bottle onto a pink candle and burn it for one hour. On the seventh day, your romantic prospect will brighten.

For luck with money, place three pennies and some pyrite, green jade, or peridot in a bottle and put it on your desk or workspace. At least three times a day, visualize a lot of money and shake the magic money bottle. After three days, your fortunes will improve.

Bowls

While a bowl is not a tool in and of itself, you can utilize bowls in your spell work often and anytime you are inspired to do so. Clear, glass bowls are regularly used.

Blessing Bowl Ritual

Just three ingredients—a red rose, a pink candle, and water—can bestow a powerful blessing. The rose signifies beauty, potential, the sunny seasons, and love for yourself and others. The candle stands for the element of Fire, the yellow flame of the rising sun in the east, harmony, higher intention, and light of the soul. Water represents its own element, flow, the direction of the west, emotions, and cleansing. This ritual can be performed alone or with a group in which you pass the bowl around.

Float the rose in a clear bowl of water and light a pink candle beside the bowl. With your left hand, gently stir the water in the bowl and say the words below.

These waters cleanse my soul and being,
Now, with a clear mind and heart, I am seeing,
I am love; my heart is as big as sky and earth.
From the east to the west, love universal gives life its worth.
Blessings to all, so mote it be.

Wand

A magical wand is a powerful tool that is used to cast the circle and invoke deities. Much like an athame, a wand focuses projects and directs energy. Because it gathers and stores magical power, a wand is wonderful for healing and can be the device with which you draw the shape when you cast the circle.

If possible, find your wand in a serendipitous manner. Draw it to yourself through attraction. A wand makes a mighty gift. If it feels really right to you, you can and should purchase your own wand. Just be sure to purify it, cleansing the energy of the shop so it is truly yours. However, before you take off for the next metaphysical five-and-dime, take a walk in the woods closest to where you reside. You may very well find the wand of your dreams waiting for you on the forest floor. Some folks prefer "live" wood such as cherry, willow, or oak branches that need to be cut off the tree. As a card-carrying eco-pagan, I vastly prefer fallen branches that nature has already harvested. Magical metals—copper, gold, and silver—are excellent for ornamenting your wand, and you may also want to adorn it with gems and crystals. The most important factor for any wand is how it "feels" in your hand. You will know immediately when you have found the right one.

Athame

Pronounced "a-tha-may," this is your magical knife. It can also be a ritual dagger or sword. The athame represents and contains yang energy, the male aspect of the deities. Ritual knives are also associated with the element of Fire. For these two reasons, your ritual knife should be placed on the right side of your altar. It is to be used to direct the energies raised in your circles and spellwork; because it is not used for cutting but rather for the manipulation of the forces involved in the work of enchantment, an athame is usually a dull blade.

The knives you use to slice bread and chop veggies are in a completely different category.

Some Wiccan traditionalists specify that the handle of the athame should be black or very dark in color (as in the artwork, left), since black is the color that absorbs energies and, therefore, becomes quickly attuned to the practitioner.

Bolline

A bolline, pronounced "bowl-in," is most often a white-handled knife (as in the artwork, left) that is used for making other tools and for cutting materials such as cords and herbs within the sacred circle. You can create your own magic wand, for example, by cutting a tree branch with your bolline. This increases the energy held within the wand and creates a magical tool by using a magical tool. You can also use your bolline for carving symbols and names into your candles and wands as well as your other tools. A bolline generally has a curved blade and a white handle to distinguish it from the athame, and it is also associated with male energy.

Candles

The popularity of candles has reached an all-time high. Candles are used by folks from all walks of life for relaxation, meditation, aromatherapy, and, most importantly, to achieve that "peaceful homey" feeling of being in your own sanctuary. This simple yet profound tool can make powerful magic. Take a moment and notice how candlelight transforms a dark room and fills the atmosphere with the energy of magical light. Suddenly the potential for transformation is evident.

A QUICK GUIDE TO CANDLE-COLOR MAGIC

 Green: money, prosperity, growth, luck, jobs, gardening, youth, beauty, fertility

 Dark blue: change, flexibility, the unconscious, psychic powers, emotional healing

 Pink: love, friendship, kindness, faithfulness, goodness, affection

 Brown: home, animal wisdom, grounding, physical healing

Black: banishes, absorbs, expels the negative, heals serious illness

 Gold: solar magic, money, attraction, the astral plane

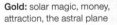 **Orange:** the law of attraction, success with legal issues, mutability, stimulation, support, encouragement, joy

 Light blue: patience, happiness, triumph over depression, calm, deep understanding, compassion

 Red: strength, protection, sexuality, vitality, passion, courage, heart, intense feelings of love, good health, power

White: purification, peace, protection from negativity, truth, binding, sincerity, serenity, chastity, gladness, spirit

 Purple: female power, stress relief, ambition, healing past wounds, goddess-hood, business success

Gray: neutrality, impasses, cancellation

Yellow: mental power and vision, intelligence, clear thinking, study, self-assurance, prosperity, divination, psychism, abundance, wisdom, the power of persuasion, charisma, a sound sleep

Every candle contains all four elements:

Air—Oxygen feeds and fans the candle flame

Earth—Solid wax forms the body of the candle

Water—Melting wax represents the fluid elemental state

Fire—The flame sparks and blazes

How to Charge a Candle

Charging a candle means instilling it with magical intent.
A candle that has been charged fills your personal space with
intention and expands it into all four elements and into the
celestial sphere. Ritual candles are chosen for their color
correspondences and are carved, "dressed," or anointed with
special oils chosen for their particular energy.

Once you clarify your intention, cleanse your candles by
passing them through the purifying smoke of sage or incense.
Further charge your candle by carving a symbol into the wax.
You can warm the tip of your ritual knife using a lit match and
carve your full intention into the candle wax. As you engrave the
appropriate magical works onto the candle, you are charging it
with energy and the hope and purpose of your spell. Some highly
successful examples of this that I have used and witnessed in
circle gatherings are: "Healing for my friend who is in the
hospital; she will recover with renewed and increased health."
"I get the raise I am asking for, and more!" "New true love enters
my life in the coming season, blessed be."

Next, you should "dress" your candle with a specific oil. Every essential oil is imbued with a power that comes from the plants and flowers of which it is made. You can also use oils to anoint yourself at the crown of the head or at the third eye to increase mental clarity. By using the inherent powers of essential oils and anointing both your tool and yourself, you are increasing and doubling the energies, in this case the candle and yourself.

Essential oils are highly concentrated extracts of flowers, herbs, roots, or resin extract, sometimes diluted in neutral-base oil. Try to ensure you are using natural oils instead of manufactured, chemical-filled perfume oil; the synthetics lack real energy. Also, approach oils with caution and don't get them in your eyes. Clean cotton gloves are a good idea to keep in your witch's kitchen for handling sensitive materials. You can avoid any mess and protect your magical tools by using oil droppers. Do not use essential oils in the first trimester of pregnancy and consult an aromatherapist if using in the later stages. Find a trusted herbalist at your local metaphysical shop; usually they can offer much in the way of helpful knowledge. I have included as much as I can in the following at-a-glance guide to oils.

Magical Meanings of Essential Oils

* Healing: bay, cedar wood, cilantro (coriander), cinnamon, eucalyptus, juniper, lime, rose, sandalwood, spearmint

* Prosperity: aloe, basil, cinnamon, clove, ginger, nutmeg, oakmoss, orange, patchouli, peppermint, pine

* Love: apricot, basil, chamomile, cilantro (coriander), clove, copal, geranium, jasmine, lemon, lime, neroli, rose, rosemary, ylang-ylang

* Sexuality: amber, cardamom, clove, lemongrass, olive, patchouli, rose

* Peace: chamomile, lavender

* Luck: nutmeg, orange, rose, vervain

* Courage: black pepper, frankincense, geranium

* Joy: bergamot, lavender, neroli, vanilla

* Divination: camphor, clove, orange

* Astral projection: benzoin, cinnamon, jasmine, sandalwood

* Dispelling negative energy and spirits: basil, clove, copal, frankincense, juniper, myrrh, peppermint, pine, rosemary, Solomon's seal, vervain, yarrow

* Protection: anise, bay, black pepper, cedar wood, clove, copal, cypress, eucalyptus, frankincense, juniper, lavender, lime, myrrh, rose geranium, sandalwood, vetiver

* Enchantment: amber, apple, ginger, tangerine

Censer

A censer, pronounced "sen-ser" and also known as a thurible, is an incense burner and represents the elements of Air and Fire. Place your incense at the very center of your altar. Incense is a way to bless your space and also to purify with the sacred smoke—your tools, your ritual circle, your mind.

The evocative scent and soft, billowing smoke will transport you in a sensory way. Nowadays, there is an incredible variety of incense burners available, so follow your instincts as to what is best for your kitchen altar—perhaps a smoking dragon or a goddess holding the fiery embers of your incense would add greatly to the energy of your altar.

Test your incense before using it in ritual, especially before organizing a group circle, to see how much smoke is produced to avoid any problems; and check with your fellow participants to make sure no one has any special sensitivities. One of my dearest and nearest gets migraines whenever any amber is used—candles, oils, incense. If you find you can't burn incense for any such reason, you can use another Air symbol instead, such as feathers, potpourri, fresh flowers, or even a paper fan.

Incense itself contains inherent energies that you can use to augment your intention and further power your magical purpose.

I have learned much about different kinds of incense—loose, cone, stock, and cylinder, as well as the best kinds of herbs to use from experimentation, asking elders, and observing magic at work. The following are two of my favorite incense recipes.

Circle Incense

4 parts frankincense

2 parts myrrh

2 parts benzoin

1 part sandalwood

1 part cinnamon

1 part rose petals

1 part vervain

1 part rosemary

1 part bay leaf

1 part orange peel

This incense will significantly aid the formation of the sphere of energy that is the ritual circle (see page 32).

Each part is a heaping teaspoon in my recipes but you can change that if you are making larger batches. A fine grind of all the ingredients is the key to good incense, so you should add a pestle and mortar to your kitchen if you plan to make a lot of incense.

Clearing Incense

This is an optimal mixture of essences to purify your home or sacred working space. Negative energics are vanquished and the path is cleared for ritual. Open windows and doors when you are burning this cleaning incense so the negative energies are released outside and dissipate. It is advisable to use this recipe if there are arguments or any other kind of disruptions in your home. Using this incense can help create sanctuary.

3 parts myrrh
3 parts copal
3 parts frankincense
1 part sandalwood

Book of Shadows

Here we have your kitchen witch's recipe record, a ledger for all your magical workings, including spells, rituals, and results. This is your journal of all you have practiced and wrought as well as your research. Are your spells more effective during the new moon in the water signs of Cancer, Pisces, or Scorpio? That may well be unique to you and as you arrive at these important discoveries, you should write them down in your Book of Shadows so you know your true power as tested by time. This is not just a ledger though, it is a living document that you can apply to magical workings to come and will even help you design your own spells and ritual recipes. All the astrology, herb lore, crystal properties, lunar signs, and seasonal information will come into play as you experiment and uncover what works best for you. By keeping my own Book of Shadows, I concluded that, for me, the new moon in Pisces is a super-powered time for my spells.

This is a book you will turn to again and again and your Book of Shadows should be very appealing to you. It can be a gorgeous, one-of-a-kind volume made with handmade paper and uniquely tooled bindings, or it can be a simple three-ring binder. Whatever is most useful to you.

A Magic Circle

When you create a sacred space and use your magical tools in it, you are leaving behind the mundane. Your kitchen is a space where you will make much magic and, despite the hurly-burly of the daily world around us, you can touch the sacrosanct. There is no need to ascend to the top of a holy mountain; anywhere you choose can be an arena of enchantment to cast the circle.

The magic circle is created by "casting," or drawing in the air with concentrated energy. Inside this circle, energy is raised, rituals are performed, and spells are worked. This consecrated space is also where you call upon the gods and goddesses and become attuned to your own special deities.

With attention and focus, working in the circle can be a wonderfully intense experience. All your senses will come alive. You will feel, see, and hear the energies you invoke. You will have created a tangible sphere of power.

You can, and doubtlessly will, cast a circle anywhere—out in the forest, on a beach, or in the comfort of your home. Wherever the circle is cast, that space becomes your temple. In your kitchen, stack the chairs against the wall to define the limits of your circle. Wiccan tradition specifies that the circle must have a diameter of nine feet (2.75m). We urban pagans might have less space, so you can extend into the closest room. I have had kitchens that more closely resembled large closets, so I would expand into the dining area and living room.

The more rooms that are blessed, the better, I say! When you work outdoors with a large group of people, very large circles are cast. Many a witch casts a circle at the beginning of any spellwork and to enclose every sabbat celebration.

Casting a magical circle is only limited by your imagination or the purpose you ascribe to it. The magic begins at your will and with your hallowed tools. To be fully imbued with energy, your tools of magic and ritual should reside on your kitchen altar. Always cleanse and purify your newly acquired tools, whether they are antique or brand new. Think of your ritual tools as energy conductors that absorb and project the energy of the environment and the ritual work you perform. So, keep them clean, clear, and positive.

Coming Full Circle

"The human heart longs for ritual—to be fully alive and whole. We must engage in rites of passage."

the kitchen altar

Your personal altar is the ideal place to incubate your ideas, your hopes, and your intentions. It can become a touchstone for morning blessings and simple daily rituals. As you evolve, so will your altar. It will become an outward expression of your inner life, your spiritual growth, and inspire you to commune with the deepest parts of yourself. An altar is where you honor the rhythms of the season as well as the rhythms of your own life. Your altar is a center for enchantment in your home, where you connect with the sacred each and every day. Creating and augmenting your holy shrine is one of the most self-nurturing acts you can perform. When mind, body, and spirit align, there is nothing more magical.

Your Personal Power Center

Before there were temples and churches, the primary place for expressing reverence was the altar. The word "altar" comes from the Latin, meaning "high." With a personal altar, you can reach the heights of your spiritual ascension in wisdom. You construct an altar when you assemble symbolic items in a meaningful manner and focus both your attention and your intention. When you work with the combined energies of these items, you are performing a ritual. Your rituals can arise from your needs, imagination, or the seasonal and traditional ceremonies that you find in this book and others. A book from which I draw much inspiration has been Nancy Brady Cunningham's *A Book of Women's Altars*, and I love her advice to bow or place your hands on the ground in front of your altar at the beginning of ritual work and at the closing. She explains that "Grounding symbolizes the end of the ritual and signals to the mind to return to an ordinary state of awareness as you re-enter daily life." An altar is a physical point of focus for the ritual, containing items considered sacred and essential to ritual work and spiritual growth. An altar can be anything from a rock in the forest to an exquisitely carved antique table. Even using portable or temporary altars can suffice, such as a board suspended between two chairs for "rituals on the go."

Sanctuary Spell

To anoint your home and turn it into a protective shield for you and your loved ones, you can rub any of the following essential oils on your doorjambs—cinnamon, clove, dragon's blood, myrrh. Walk through the door into your home and close it securely.

Take the remaining essential oils and rub a bit on all other doors and windows. Light anointed white candles and place them in the windows and chant the words of the spell below.

My home is my temple.
Here I live and love,
Safe and secure,
Both below and above.
And so it is by magic sealed.

Creating Your Kitchen Altar

On a low table or chest of your choosing, place a forest-green cloth and a brown candle to represent family and home. Following this, add lovely objects you have gathered, including items from the garden and the outdoors: ocean-carved driftwood, a gorgeous flower, a dried seedpod, a favorite crystal—whatever pleases your eye. It is of the utmost importance to add a bouquet of wildflowers native to your area, which you should have gathered close to where you live, or bought locally.

These posies will help integrate you and your home into your neighborhood and geographic region. Add a sweetly scented sachet of herbs from your kitchen garden or those you intend to plant—for example, rosemary, lavender, thyme, or mint, all of which imbue your space with positive energy. Burn associated essential oils, choosing those which will create an aura of comfort around your kitchen, including vanilla, cinnamon, or sweet-orange neroli in an oil lamp. Finally, anoint the brown candle, concentrating on the power of peace and bliss surrounding your home and all around your kitchen altar. Chant the words below:

Peace and plenty are in abundance
And here true bliss surrounds,
From now on, all disharmony is gone,
This is a place of powerful blessings
For here lives sheer joy.
And so it is—blessed be!

This consecrated space will now ease your spirits at any time. Your altar connects you to the earth of which you are a part.

Kitchen Magic Altar Herbs

* Cinnamon refreshes and directs spirituality; it is a protection herb and handy for healing, money, love, sensuality, personal power, and success with work and creative projects.

* Clove is good for bringing money to you and for helping evade negative energies and block them.

* Lavender is a potent healer that calms and aids deep rest and dreams.

* Myrrh has been considered to be very sacred since ancient times and will intensify your spirituality. It also wards off bad spirits.

* Nutmeg is a lucky herb that promotes good health and abundance. It also encourages loyalty and marital fidelity.

* Peppermint is an herb of purification and increases psychic powers. Mint brings relaxation and can help you sleep, reducing anxiety.

* Rosemary purifies and increases memory and intelligence. This plant also heightens sensuality and bonds of love. It will also keep you youthful!

* Sage brings wisdom, health, and long life. It is very useful for dispelling negative vibrations and encouraging cleansing. Sage can help your wishes come true, too.

* Star anise aids divination and psychic abilities.
* Tonka bean will give you courage and draws love and money.
* Vanilla is an herb of love and expands and enriches your mental capacity.

Pot of Gold: Abundance Altar Blessing

Cauldron magic is more about the acts of brewing something new than it is about purification by water. To attract money, fill a big pot with fresh water and place it on your altar during the waxing moon. Pour a cup of milk, adding one tablespoon of honey and one tablespoon of ground cloves into the pot as an offering. Finally, toss a handful of dried chamomile, moss, and vervain into the vessel. With your head raised high, say aloud:

> *I call upon you, gods and goddesses of old,*
> *to fill my purse with gold.*
> *I offer you mother's milk and honey sweet.*
> *With harm to none and blessings to thee, I honor you*
> *for bringing me health and prosperity.*

Place the offering bowl on your altar and leave the aromatic mixture there to instill your kitchen with the energy of abundance. After four hours and forty-four minutes, go outside your home and pour the offering into your kitchen garden or into the roots of a shrub. Then bow in appreciation of the kindness of the gods and goddesses.

✳

FLORAL FUNDING

The following list of plants can be used in any ritual work whose intention is prosperity: allspice, almond, basil, bergamot, cedar leaves, cinnamon, cinquefoil, clover, dill, ginger, heliotrope, honeysuckle, hyssop, jasmine, mint, myrtle, nutmeg, oak moss, sassafras, vervain, and woodruff. Try these alone or in mixtures, tinctures, or grind into your incenses. You can also plant a prosperity garden and refresh your abundance altar with herbs and flowers grown by your own hand.

Salt of the Earth Blessing Spell

Every kitchen has a box of salt. This most common of seasonings is essential to physical health and also to the health of your home. With a bowl of salt alone, you can purify your home every day and have a "safe zone" for ritual work. You can leave a bowl of pure salt in any room you feel is in need of freshening; the salt absorbs negativity. Many kitchen witches use this homely approach on a daily basis early in the day, tidying up and cleansing energy to charge the home with some positivity.

In your kitchen, take a bowl of water, freshly drawn, along with a small cup of salt. Take the vessel of water and sprinkle in as much salt as you feel is needed. Anoint your fingers by dipping them in the salt water and then touch the middle of your forehead around your third eye.

Now turn to the east and say:

Power of the East,
Source of the Sun rising,
Bring me new beginnings.

After speaking, sprinkle some of the salt water within the eastern part of your kitchen.

Then face south and say:

> *Source of the Starry Cross,*
> *Place of warmth and light,*
> *Bring me joy and bounty.*

Scatter droplets of salt water within the southern direction. Face the west and speak aloud:

> *Powers of the West,*
> *Source of oceans, mountains, and deserts all,*
> *Bring me the security of the ground beneath my feet.*

Scatter some droplets within the west side of your kitchen. Face north now and speak aloud:

> *Powers of the North,*
> *Bringer of winds and the polestar,*
> *Show me vision and insight.*

Sprinkle some salt water within the northern area of the room.

End this ritual by sprinkling water and salt all around your home, especially around windows, sills, doorways, and thresholds where energy passes in and out as visitors and delivery people come and go. In this way, you are cleansing and managing the energy of your space. After a stressful occurrence, you can repeat this ritual and then leave a bowl of salt out for 24 hours so it can rid your sacred space of negative "vibes."

Kitchen Warming Spell

When you or a friend move into a new home, place a wreath on the front door and also on the outside of the kitchen or back door (if your kitchen doesn't lead directly outside). Gather two bundles of dried hops or eucalyptus, tie them with green and brown ribbons, and hang them high on the door. Walk through each door with a brown candle in a glass votive jar and aromatic cinnamon incense. Intone these words:

House of my body, I accept your shelter.
Home of my heart, I receive your blessings.
Home of my heart, I am open to joy.
And so it is. And so it shall be.

Witching Hour Altar for Well-Being

Creating a health altar will safeguard your physical health and that of your loved ones. Your altar is a sacred workspace and, in this case, a place of potent and practical magic. Set up your healing altar facing north, the direction associated with the energy of manifestation. North is also the direction of the midnight hour, sometimes known as the "Witching Hour."

Find a pure white square of fabric to drape over your altar for clean and clear new beginnings. Take two green candles and place them in green glass holders and position them in the two farthest corners. Place your censer in between and burn sandalwood, camphor, or frankincense for purification. You can adorn your altar with objects that connote well-being to you. Perhaps an amethyst candleholder with purple candles, a bowl of bright red apples from your backyard, a dwarf lemon tree bursting with the restorative power of Vitamin C, a crock of curative salts from the sea. These symbolic items and any others you select will imbue your altar with the magic that lives inside of you and your intention toward good health. It is imperative that the altar be pleasing to your eye and fill you with gladness when you gaze upon it. After you perform midnight-hour rituals there for a while, a positive healing energy field will radiate from your altar. Blessed be!

Power Potpourri

¼ cup (5g) dried rosemary

4 dried bay laurel leaves

⅛ cup (5g) dried sage

1 teaspoon dried juniper berries

Simmer this mixture in a pot of water on your stove whenever you feel the need to infuse your space with protection or want an energetic turnaround from negative to positive. A bad day at work, family squabble, or an unfortunate incident in your neighborhood: instead of just muddling along, you can do something about it, and your creation of the positive will help you and your loved ones as well as your neighbors. Be sure to set your intention before gathering the herbs from your stores.

✳
SEASONAL ALTARS

One of the most vital ways pagans can keep in touch with nature is through the creation of seasonal altars. Your altar helps you to maintain balance in your life and deepen your spiritual connection to the world around you. A seasonal altar is your tool for ceremonies to honor Mother Nature and receive the deep wisdom of the earth by blending the energies of the season. Choose items relating to the current season— shells, feathers, leaves, flowers, and herbs—and add them to your altar. Your periodic altars are the middle ground between Earth and sky, the meeting point of the four elements. Creating these altars is very life-affirming.

Mix the herbs together by hand. While you are sifting them through your fingers, close your eyes and visualize your home protected by a boundary of glowing white light. Imagine the light running through you to the herbs in your hand and charging them with the energy of safety, sanctity, and protection. Add the herbs to slowly simmering water and breathe in the newly charged air.

Burning Away Bad Luck

Your kitchen is the heart of your home, your sanctuary. Yet the world is constantly coming in and bringing mundane energy over your threshold—problems at the workplace, financial woes, bad news from your neighborhood or the world at large. All this negativity wants to get in the way and stay. While you can't do anything about the stock market crash in China or a co-worker's divorce, you can do something about not allowing this bad energy to cling to you by using this home-keeping spell. The best times to release any and all bad luck are on a Friday 13th or on any waxing moon. As you know, Friday 13th is considered a lucky day on the witch's calendar.

Get a big black candle and a black crystal, a piece of white paper, a black pen with black ink, and a cancellation stamp, readily available at any stationery store. Go into your backyard or a nearby park or woodlands and find a flat rock that has a

slightly concave surface. Using the pen, write down on the white paper that of which you want to rid yourself and your home; this will be your release request. Place the candle and the black crystal on the rock; light the candle, and while it burns, intone the following spell:

"The more use an altar gets, the more energy it builds up, making your spells even more effective and powerful."

Waxing moon, most wise Selene,
From me this burden please dispel
Upon this night so clear and bright
I release ___ to the moon tonight.

Visualize a clear and peaceful home filled with only positivity as the candle burns for 13 minutes. Stamp the paper with the cancel stamp. Snuff the candle, fold the paper away from your body, and place it under the rock. Speak your thanks to the moon for assisting you. If you have a truly serious issue at hand, repeat the process for 13 nights and all will be vanquished.

brewing up blessings

Witch's brews are one of the most important aspects of house magic. These tonics comprise many kinds of teas, wines, ciders, and refreshments as well as medicinal tinctures, tisanes, infusions, and herbal vinegars. Your garden grows plants, herbs, and fruits that are the source of delectable draughts and healing concoctions, which are at the very heart of kitchen witchery. A pantry filled with bottles of brews made by your own hand will be a constant source of delight to you and your inner circle.

A Mug of Magic

The British and kitchen witches have one thing in common—
they believe a good pot of tea can fix almost anything. And it is
true—heartache, headaches, and all manner of ills seem to
evaporate in the steam that rises from the spout of the kettle.
With a handful of herbs and a cauldron-full of witchy wisdom,

big healing can result from a small cup of tea.
Once you have the knack of that, you can
also brew up simples, digestives, tisanes,
tonics, tinctures, and the many other
concoctions that can be created right at
home. This is one of the most delightful
aspects of kitchen witchery as these
recipes are usually easy enough as long
as you have all of the proper ingredients.
They make all the difference after a long day
at the office; they can be enjoyed alone and can also be shared to
great effect. Bottled and hand labeled, these potions also make
significant gifts that will be long remembered for the
thoughtfulness as well as the delight and comfort received.
Prepare to brew up much joy.

Simples

Teas brewed from a single herb are commonly called simples, a lovely phrase from olden times. Experience has taught me that simples often have the most potency; the purity of that single plant essence can come through undiluted. This book contains plenty of herbs you can use to brew tasty, helpful, and healing simples, but yarrow is one you should definitely brew regularly. Boil 2½ cups (590ml) of spring water. Place a half-ounce (15ml) of dried yarrow into your favorite crockery pot and pour over the water. Steep for 10 minutes and strain with a non-metallic implement, such as an inexpensive bamboo strainer or cheesecloth. Sweeten with honey; clover honey intensifies the positivity of this potion and makes it a supremely lucky drink. Yarrow brings courage, heart, and is a major medicine. All these aspects make yarrow one of the most strengthening of all simples.

Jasmine Joy Ritual

Jasmine tea is a delightful concoction and can create an aura of bliss and conviviality. It is available at any grocer or purveyor of organic goods, but homegrown is even better. Brew a cup of jasmine tea and let it cool. Add two parts lemonade to one part jasmine tea and drink the mixture with a good friend. Jasmine is a vine and represents the intertwining of people. You will be more bonded to anyone with whom you share this sweet ritual.

This is also a tonic that you can indulge in when alone. I recommend brewing up a batch every Monday, or "Moon Day," to ensure that each week is filled with joyfulness.

As the jasmine tea steeps, pray:

On this Moon Day in this new week,
I call upon the spirits to guide joy to my door.
By this moon on this day, I call upon Selene, goddess fair
To show me the best way to live.
For this, I am grateful.
Blessed be the brew; blessed be me.

✴

TELEPATHY TEA

The humble dandelion, abhorred by lawn keepers everywhere, hides its might very well. Dandelion root tea can call upon the spirit of anyone whose advice you might need. Simply place a freshly brewed simple using this herbal root on your bedroom altar or nightstand. Before you sleep, say the name of your helper aloud seven times. In a dream or vision, the spirit will visit you and answer all your questions. During medieval times, this spell was used to find hidden treasure. Chaucer, who was well-versed in astrology and other metaphysics, advised this tried and true tea.

Dandelion Divination Wine

14 ounces (400g) freshly picked and cleaned dandelion blossoms (no stems or leaves)

1 orange and 1 lemon, thinly sliced

1 gallon (3.8 liters) water, heated to boiling

3 pounds (1.35kg) organic sugar

1 piece of dried bread

½ ounce (15g) dry yeast

One woman's weed is another's prized secret for myriad mystical uses— delectable sautéed greens and mixed salads and therapeutic teas as well as a very special kind of wine. Of course, hedge witches have known for centuries that this hardy specimen can be used for calling upon helpful spirits, dispelling negative energy, and bringing good luck. One of the most important uses of this herb is divination, making this wine an absolutely enchanting way to foresee the future.

Place the flowers in a very large bowl that can handle heat; place the orange and lemon slices on top of the flowers and pour in the hot water. Cover the bowl with a clean, dry towel and place on a pantry shelf for ten days. Strain the mixture into a different bowl and spoon in the sugar, stirring to dissolve. Toast the bread and then spread the yeast on top, then let it float on top of your mixture. Cover and let sit for another three days.

Strain the liquid and compost the bread and any flower remains. Bottle your dandelion wine in special bottles, cork, and label it. This is a marvelous libation to share during Wiccan holidays and anytime you are in need of a positive portent.

In Vino Veritas: Visionary Wine

Marigolds are said to lend prophetic powers and more; you can even make a wine using the exact same recipe for dandelion wine (see left), but make sure to pick the marigolds when the flowers have fully opened by the heat and light of the sun. Drink the marigold wine when you desire to have prophetic visions and record them. This could become part of a yearly ritual for solar new years, otherwise known as birthdays. Celebrate and commemorate these dreams and visions as vital information could come as result— after all, in wine, truth.

Pantry Power

Many enthusiasts enjoy several cups a day of their favorite herbal infusion, which is a large portion of herb brewed for at least four hours and as long as ten. I recommend one cup of the dried herb placed in a quart-canning jar and filled with freshly boiled water. After the steeping, strain using a non-metallic method, such as cheesecloth or bamboo. Herbal infusions can be made with the leaves and fruits that provide the magical and healing aspects of this comforting concoction. Many of the favorite kitchen witch herbs contain minerals, antioxidants, and phytochemicals. Roots, leaves, flowers, needles, and seeds can all be used—depending on which fruit or herb is chosen to be the base. There are some cases when all parts of the plant can be used in some manner, and for others only one or two parts are safe—it is important, when creating a blend from scratch, to research the ingredients to understand what parts can be used.

What do you need to attend to in your life right now? This list of herbs and associations can be your guide; one of the smartest ways to approach this methodology is to brew right before bedtime and you will awaken to a freshly infused herb. Here I've listed some of the most popular herbs and fruits used to create infusions.

* Anise seeds and leaves soothe cramps and aches
* Caraway seeds aid in romantic issues and help with colic
* Catnip leaves increase attractiveness

* Chamomile flowers help with sleep and are good for abundance
* Dandelion leaves make wishes come true
* Echinacea makes the body strong
* Ginseng root increases men's vigor
* Nettle leaves are good for lung function and hex breaking
* Peppermint leaves rid tummy discomfort and are cleansing
* Pine needles increase skin health as well as financial health
* Rose hip fruit is packed with Vitamin C and can halt colds and flu
* Sage leaves purify energy and are a natural antibiotic
* Skullcap leaves cures insomnia, headaches, anxiety, and nervous tension
* St.-John's-wort leaves act as an anti-depressant and can provide protection
* Thyme leaves are antiseptic and a protectant
* Yarrow flowers reduce fever and can bring courage and good luck

Cinnamon Liqueur

1 cup (240ml) vodka

2 cloves

1 teaspoon ground
coriander seed

1 cinnamon stick

1 cup (240ml) simple
sugar syrup (see below)

This popular pagan beverage gives peppy energy and can also be a love potion. These few ingredients can lead to a lifetime of devotion.

Pour the vodka into a bowl and add the herbs. Cover with a clean, dry towel and place in a cupboard for two weeks. Strain and filter until the result is a clear liquid into which you add the simple syrup and place back on the shelf for a week. Store this in a pink- or red-capped bottle; you now have liquid love. You can add this to hot chocolate, water, tea, or milk for a delightful drink to share with a partner.

✳
DIY ELIXIR

You can make a simple syrup, a base for any liqueur, in five short minutes by boiling 1 cup (200g) of sugar in ½ cup (120ml) of water.

Passion Potion Spell

Lower the lamps, light red candles, and enjoy a warm cup of cocoa with a shot of the cinnamon liqueur. Speak this spell aloud as you are preparing the libation—you will radiate passion and draw your lover to you with this enchantment:

Today, I awaken the goddess in me.

By surrendering to my love
for thee.

Tonight, I will heat the
night with my fire.

As we drink this cup,
we awaken desire.

I am alive! I am love.
So mote it be.

Coming Full Circle

"I love how all-encompassing the creation of magic potions can be: you start with a handful of seeds, tend your herb garden, and end up with a pantry filled with libations that are at once medicinal, delicious, celebratory, and, most importantly, crafted with loving care."

kitchen cupboard cures

Centuries ago, every village depended on "medicine women"—wise crones who used the knowledge handed down to them as healers. While we now live in an age of modern medicine, there is still much you can do using the natural remedies right from your pantry and kitchen garden. The roses blooming by your front gate contain more vitamins than the expensive bottle of chemicals on your shelf. Your home-brewed honey vinegar is a powerful tonic your family will love. Inside your cupboard, a magical world awaits with which you can conjure much health and happiness.

The Homely Healing Arts

For me, witchcraft was and is the most natural thing in the world—and indeed it is all about being in the natural world. On woodland walks, my Aunt Edith pointed out nettles, wild mint, Queen Anne's lace, and other herbs that grew by creek beds near my home. We picked, steeped, and sipped concoctions we made together as she imparted her homely wisdom. Little did I know at the time that I was being gently schooled as an apprentice kitchen witch.

Modern life and its many pressures has us feeling more stressed than ever. Yet how often do you see a stressed-out witch? Rarely, I assure you.

We witches also have to keep pace with the modern world, but our connection to the earth and the cycles of nature helps maintain balance and harmony. This chapter is aimed at conjuring wellness so you can stay centered, grounded, and healthy. When our grandmothers and elders tended cuts, bruises, colds, or other illnesses, they didn't have a corner drugstore. Instead, they relied on simple wisdom, common sense, and well stocked pantries.

These preparations were made from plants that grew in the kitchen garden or from foraged wild weeds. This collection of kitchen-cupboard cures combines the wisdom of our elders with a modern kitchen witch's sensibilities.

With these, you will begin to learn what works for you and master the art of self-care as you bring comfort to your loved ones. Here are tips and kitchen-witch secrets to healing many maladies and feeling your best every day, come rain or shine.

Lavender Space-Clearing Spell

To do any healing work, you must first clear clutter, both physical and otherwise, that creates energy blocks. Banish "stale" and unhealthy energy from your kitchen workspace and living space with this herbal magic. Steep lavender in hot water; once the infusion has cooled to room temperature, dip your fingertips in it and sprinkle tiny droplets throughout your home while intoning these words:

All is new here now, I say.
Make way, be gone, goodbye
All here is new, say I.
So mote it be!

Use the remainder of the lavender infusion to wash your front steps or stoop—the entry to your sanctuary—thereby clearing and cleansing the threshold of your home. You will notice that every time you enter your home, it feels lighter and brighter, this is thanks to the energetic de-cluttering.

Breathe Easy Spell

10 drops rosemary
10 drops tea tree
10 drops eucalyptus
10 drops lavender
1 teaspoon sea salt

Banish colds and coughs or keep them at bay with this sweet-smelling spell. In a blue bottle, shake together all the ingredients.

Hold the container in both hands under your nose and inhale deeply three times. After the last exhalation, intone:

Power of wind,
Strength of the trees,
Energy of the earth,
Salts of the sea,
I call upon you to keep me well and strong.
With harm to none, so mote it be.

You can administer this respiratory booster with four drops added to the water of a vaporizer or diffuser or a cotton ball tucked into your pillowcase. Six drops poured into the running water of a hot bath will ease breathing immediately.

✳
ESSENTIAL OILS FOR COMMON AILMENTS

Use these oils in bath water, diffusers, dabbed onto pulse points, or sprays to infuse your home with the healing vitality of these plant essences.

Allergies: chamomile, melissa

Headaches: geranium, lavender, linden, peppermint

Immune boosters: hyssop, jasmine, rose, thyme

Insomnia: clary sage, hops, lavender

Colds and flu: eucalyptus, lavender, pine, thyme

Tummy troubles: basil, chamomile, peppermint

Cramps: linden, sunflower, yarrow

Arthritis: eucalyptus, marjoram, pine, rosemary

Fatigue: bergamot, clary sage, neroli, rose

Heart's Ease Cauldron Cure

1 ounce (28g) dried rosehips

1 ounce (28g) dried hibiscus

2 ounces (56g) dried mint

1 tablespoon dried ginger root

Here is a soothing sip that can uplift your spirits anytime and also serves to ward off chills. This combination of herbs brings about the "letting go" of sorrows, worries, and doubts, and reignites feelings of self-love.

Stir all the ingredients together in a clean cauldron to mix. Pour into a colored jar, and seal the lid tightly.

✳

MOTHER NATURE'S MULTIVITAMIN

Once a rose has bloomed and all petals have fallen away, the hip is ready to be picked. Ground rose hips are the best source of immune-boosting Vitamin C; they contain 50 percent more Vitamin C than oranges. One tablespoon provides more than the recommended daily adult allowance of 90 mg for men and 75 mg for women. The pulp from rose hips may be used in sauces or made into jelly. What a delicious way to ward off colds and ailments!

When you are ready to brew, pour hot water over the herbs, two teaspoons per cup. While this steeps for 5 minutes, write down on a small piece of paper any thoughts or fears of which you need to rid yourself. Now say each one aloud, then chant, "Begone!" After this letting-go ritual, burn the paper together with sage in the cauldron on your altar. As you sip the tea, enjoy your renewed sense of self and peace of mind.

Handmade Herbal Amulet

You will experience years of enjoyment from tending your garden, as Voltaire taught us in his masterpiece, *Candide*. You can share that pleasure with your friends and those you love with gifts from your garden. Your good intentions will be returned many times over. I keep a stock of small muslin drawstring bags for creating amulets. If you are a crafty kitchen witch, you can make the bags, sewing them by hand, and stuff the dried herbs inside.

Amulets should be kept on your person at all times, in a pocket, in your purse or book bag, or placed on a string around your neck.

* For courage and heart: mullein or borage
* For good cheer: nettle or yarrow
* For fellow witches: ivy, broomstraw, maidenhair fern
* For safe travels: comfrey
* For fertility: cyclamen or mistletoe

Conjuring by the Cup

Tea is not only a delectable drink, but also of equal importance are the great healing powers contained in each cup. Growing and drying herbs for your own kitchen-witchery brews is truly one of life's simple pleasures. Tea conjures a very powerful alchemy because, when you drink it, you take the magic inside of you. For an ambrosial brew with the power to calm any storm, add a sliver of ginger root and a teaspoon each of chamomile and peppermint to two cups of boiling water. Let steep and, as the mixture brews and cools, pray using the words below.

This day I pray for strength and health,
And the wisdom to see the beauty in each waking moment.
Blessings abound; good health is true wealth.

Green Witchery Healthy Brews

Herbal tea nourishes the soul, heals the body, and calms the mind. Try any of the following:

* Blackberry leaf tea reduces mood swings, evens glucose levels, thus aiding weight management. This miraculous herbal even helps circulation and aids such issues as inflammation and varicose veins. It is helpful to cancer patients and is believed to be a preventative.

* Catnip is one of the witchiest of teas. At the first inkling of a sore throat or impending cold, drink a warm cup of catnip tea and head off to bed. You will awaken feeling much better. Catnip soothes the nervous system and can safely help get a restless child go off to sleep as it's a gentle sleep-inducer.

* Cardamom is a favorite of expectant mothers as it calms nausea and morning sickness; this east-India fragrant is excellent for digestion, clears and cleans your mouth and throat. If you like cinnamon you will love cardamom.

* Nettle raises your energy level, boosts the immune system, and is packed with iron and vitamins.

* Fennel is excellent for awakening and uplifting and is great for digestion and cleansing. Fennel also is an excellent natural breath freshener.

* Echinacea lends an increased and consistent sense of well-being and prevents colds and flu. It is a very powerful immune booster.

* Ginger root calms and cheers while aiding digestion and nausea and can also fend off coughs and sore throats.

* Dandelion root grounds and centers, providing many minerals and nutrients. This wonderful weed is also a cleanser as well as a wholly natural detoxifier.

Simple Salt Magic

The one thing every household has in the kitchen is salt, either
plain white grains or the larger, kosher crystals. This most
common of cupboard condiments is also an essential in magic,
dating back thousands of years and used by Egyptians,
Chaldeans, Babylonians, and early European tribes for
purification, protection, and cleansing. Salt is often utilized in
hoodoo, sprinkled on doorsteps and pathways to keep bad spirits
away (as well as bad people), and added into witch bottles to
clear energy. During the era of the early Roman Empire, soldiers
were paid in salt—it was that valuable. Long have these grains
been used to preserve and improve the taste of foods.

Perhaps the highest purpose of salt is as a healer; it is essential in the diet for good health and external uses in baths and rubs can be enormously relaxing. Salt removes negative energy and can even vanquish a headache in short order with the following magical application.

Headache Healer: Salt Serenity Spell

Fill a tea kettle and set it to boil. Pour hot water into a mug and add a full tablespoon of salt. Once it has cooled to a warm temperature, hold the mug against each of your temples in turn and keep it there for a long moment. Dip your forefinger of your left hand into the salt water and gently rub each of your temples and your forehead in circular movements. Sit or lay flat in silence for some time with your eyes closed. If this turns into a nap, all the better. When you are ready, rise and your headache will be at bay. Place the cup on your kitchen altar for a period of 24 hours so it can draw out any negative energy from your home. After this, throw the salt water from the cup onto your front step or sidewalk to keep any bad juju away. As you walk down your front path, you'll notice that you feel clear-headed and peaceful.

Setting Sun Spell

The jar of bay leaf in your spice cupboard will get you one step closer to tranquility. To clear energy and prepare for a week of calm clarity, find your favorite white flower—iris, lily, rose, one that is truly beautiful to your eye. Monday's setting sun is the time for this spell, immediately after the sun goes below the horizon. Anoint a white candle with jasmine oil and place on your altar. Take your single white blossom and add that to your altar in a bowl of freshly drawn water. Place a whole bay leaf on a glass dish in front of the lit candle and speak aloud the words of the spell below.

This fire is pure; this flower is holy; this water is clear.
These elements purify me.
I walk in light with nothing in my way.
My energy is pure, my spirit is holy, my being is clear.
Blessed be.

Burn the bay leaf in the fire of the candle and put in the glass dish where it can turn into ash, smudging as it burns.

Bay Leaf Balm

Any body oil or herbal oil can be turned into a salve with the addition of wax. The ratio for a body salve is 3 ounces (90ml) coconut oil to 1 ounce (30ml) beeswax. If you have a bay laurel tree, pick some fresh leaves. You can also go to your spice rack and take three leaves from the jar and grind them in your mortar and pestle until broken up into fine, little pieces. Set aside a fourth whole leaf. Use a double boiler to heat the oil and wax until completely melted. Test the viscosity of your salve by pouring a dab onto a cold plate. If satisfied with the consistency, pour off into clean jars to cool. If you need to add more wax, now is the time to do it. Balms are simply salves with the addition of essential oils. Add two drops of eucalyptus essential oil and two drops of lemon oil while the mix is still warm. Sprinkle in the finely crushed bay laurel, stir well, and seal to preserve the aroma.

Bay leaf balm will have a wonderfully calming effect anytime you use it and can be rubbed on your temples when you need to de-stress. I recommend Sunday night soaks, where you slather on the balm before stepping into a hot bath. Take a washcloth and massage your skin, then lie back and relax for 20 long minutes. When you drain the bathtub, your stress will also empty out, and you can start your week afresh, ready to handle anything that comes your way.

Body Purification Ritual Bath

Since the time of the ancients in the Mediterranean and Mesopotamia, salts of the sea combined with soothing oils have been used to purify the body by way of gentle, ritualized rubs. From Bathsheba to Cleopatra, these natural salts have been used to smooth the skin and enhance circulation, which is vital to overall physical health as skin is the single largest organ in the human body. Dead Sea salts have long been a popular export and are readily available at most health food shops and spas. You can make your own salts, however, and not only control the quality and customize the scent, but save money, too. The definitive benefit that is far above the cost savings is that you can imbue your concoction with your intention, which is absolutely imperative when you are performing rites of self-healing,

Shekinah's Garden of Eden Salts

3 cups (385g) Epsom salts

½ cup (120ml) sweet almond oil

1 tablespoon glycerin

4 drops ylang-ylang essential oil

2 drops jasmine essential oil

Shekinah translates to "She who dwells within" and is the Hebrew name for the female aspect of God. Olden legend has it that she co-created the world side by side with Yahweh, the god of Israel. This simple recipe recalls the scents and primal memories of that edenic paradise.

Mix well and store in a colored, well-capped glass bottle. Prepare by lighting citrus-and rose-scented candles. Step out of your clothes and hold the salts in the palms of your hand. Pray aloud:

> *Shekinah, may your wisdom guide me,*
> *My body is a temple to you.*
> *Here I worship today, with heart and hands,*
> *Body and soul.*
> *I call upon you for healing,*
> *Shekinah, bring me breath and life.*
> *Ancient one, I thank you*
> *With heart and hands,*
> *Body and soul.*

Use these salts with a clean washcloth or new sponge and gently scrub your body while standing in the shower or bathtub. The ideal time is during a waxing morning moon or at midnight during a new moon. You will glow with health and inner peace.

Saffron Serenity Spell

This evening ritual is a wonderful way to end the day. Light a yellow candle for mental clarity, and anoint it with calming and uplifting bergamot oil. Place a yellow rose in a vase to the left of the candle. To the right, place a bowl containing at least two citrine or quartz crystals.

Saffron water is made by boiling a single teaspoon of saffron from your cupboard in 2 quarts (2 liters) of distilled water. Let cool to room temperature and pour into the bowl of crystals. Put your hands together as in prayer and dip your hands in the bowl. Touch your third eye in the center of your forehead, anointing yourself with the saffron water. Now, speak aloud:

Goddess great, fill me with your presence
This night, I am whole and at peace.
Breathing in, breathing out, I feel your safe embrace.
And so it is.

The Serenity Spectrum

I have already explained how powerful candles can be (see page 23), but did you know you can burn colored candles on certain days of the week for all kinds of well-being? The guide below shows which candles to use and when.

* For inner peace, burn silver candles on Monday.

* To let go of anger, burn orange candles on Tuesday.

* For mental clarity, burn yellow candles on Wednesday.

* For a peaceful home, burn blue candles on Thursday.

* For kindness and compassion, burn pink candles on Friday.

* For success at work and for physical well-being, burn green candles on Friday.

* To overcome regret or guilt, burn white candles on Saturday.

* For self-confidence and to overcome fear, burn red candles on Sunday.

Coming Full Circle

"Every day, you can renew your own health and wellness in many small ways; a cup of green tea with a morning prayer can be a simple rite that gives you calm and greater wellness."

chapter 5

a gardener's grimoire

Gardening is one of the most creative things you can do and an exercise in mindfulness. Growing herbs to use in remedies and spellcraft is doubly rewarding; and with each passing season, you will grow in your wisdom and skill. Your garden—whether it is a balcony full of blooms or a plot out back—can be a sanctuary, a place where your spirit is renewed and restored. Tending and growing these magical herbs and potent plants is a kind of botanical alchemy; the teas, tinctures, potions, recipes, and flower essences you craft are proof that yours is an enchanted garden.

Your Magical Intent

Do you use chamomile regularly? Do you purify your space with sage? Are rosemary, mint, and lavender favorites in your sachets and teas? Think of all the herbs and plants you love and use often, then begin researching their upkeep and care. Make sure to research your planting zone so you get the optimal climate to nurture your plants and herbs. Once you have planned your plantings, infuse your plot with magical intention. Keep careful track of your progress in your Book of Shadows. As you grow in experience and expertise, so will the healing power of your plot.

Remember to research plants and herbs that can be toxic or poisonous to ensure the safety of children or our canine and feline friends. Many a beloved power flower handed down to us is excellent for magical workings but not at all appropriate for tea, edibles, or such things. Make sure visiting children stay far away from wisteria, rhododendron, lily of the valley, narcissus, foxglove,

larkspur, hydrangea, and oleander. They may be beautiful but they are deadly, literally.

Every new moon is an opportunity to sow seeds for new beginnings and deepen your magical intent. Your plantings can be a tool you use for a better life, bringing brighter health and greater abundance, as well as mindfulness and serenity. Nature is our greatest teacher and a garden is a gift through which you both give and receive.

Basil Money Magic

Harvest several leaves from your basil plants and then place them inside a clear bowl of water on your kitchen altar overnight. In the morning, remove the leaves and let them dry on your kitchen windowsill. Touch the water to your fingertips and touch your purse, wallet, and anywhere you keep money. If you handle money at your workplace, bottle some of the basil water in a tiny jar and do the same. Once the soaked leaves have dried, place one in your wallet, purse, and pockets to attract money to you and yours. It also repels thieves and protects from a loss of wealth. You can also put some basil leaves on your desk at home or work to enhance prosperity for your employer or before asking for a raise. Basil is truly a kitchen witch's boon.

Lavender Self-Blessing Ritual

The time you take to restore yourself is precious. Morning is the optimal time to perform a self-blessing, which will help you maintain your physical health and provide an emotional boost each and every day. Take a bundle of dried lavender grown in your kitchen garden or from a purveyor of organic herbs and place it into a muslin sack. Knead the lavender three times and breathe in the calming scent. Beginning at the top of your head, your crown chakra, pass the pouch all the way down to your feet, gently touching your other six sacred chakras: your forehead, throat, solar plexus, upper and lower abdomen, and pelvis. Holding the lavender bag over your heart, incant the spell below.

Gone are sorrows, illness, and woe;
Here wisdom and health flows.
My heart is whole, joy fills my soul.
Blessed be me.

Wish Upon a Waxing Moon

This spell will sanctify your garden space. When the moon is waxing, growing larger toward the phase of fullness, gather green and purple candles and anoint them with sandalwood and rose oil, respectively. To create a simple outdoor altar, place the candles on a large, flat rock or your garden wall. Place a small, potted ivy vine on the altar, along with a cup of water. Burn sandalwood incense on the northern side of your outdoor altar. Now close your eyes and meditate upon your hopes and dreams of growth—personal, business, spiritual, for loved ones. When the incense has almost completely burned, take the ivy and plant it in the optimal spot in your garden, where it can thrive and spread, creating beauty as it vines on a wall or fence. Use the cup to water the plant. Now bow and pray, using the words below.

As this living thing expands,
So shall the power of this magical space grow.
Oh, goddess of the Earth, I dedicate my magic to you.
Harm to none and only good work from this holy space.

This ivy is now a botanical "familiar" and as it flourishes, so will
you. I encourage you to continually revitalize your outdoor altar
by adorning it with sacred objects that have meaning to you:
iridescent feathers, a lovely rock from a nearby creek, a bright red
pomegranate, a perfect white rose, or anything else you find in
nature that will make a perfect offering.

New Moon Ritual: Sowing Seeds of Change

Nature is the ultimate creator. From a nearby gardening or hardware store, get an assortment of seed packets to plant newness into your life. If your thumb is not the greenest, try nasturtiums, which are extremely hardy, grow quickly, and spread, beautifying any area. They also re-seed themselves, which is a lovely bonus.

On a new-moon morning, draw a square in your yard with a "found-in-nature" wand—a fallen branch. Apartment dwellers can use a planter on the deck or a big pot for this ritual. Each corner of the square needs a candle and a special stone. I get my stones at new-age bookstores, which often have the shiny tumbled versions for as little as a dollar. Mark the corners in a clockwise fashion as follows:

* Green candle and peridot or jade for creativity, prosperity, and growth

* Orange candle and jasper or onyx for clear thinking and highest consciousness

* Blue candle and turquoise or celestine for serenity, kindness, and a happy heart

* White candle and quartz or limestone for purification and safety

Repeat the chant below as you light each candle.

Greatest Gaia, I turn to you to help me renew.
Under this new moon and in this old earth.
Blessings to you; blessings to me.
Blessed be.

Put the seeds under the soil with your fingers and tamp them down gently with your wand—the branch—which you should also stick in the ground at this time. Water your new-moon garden and affirmative change will begin in your life that very day.

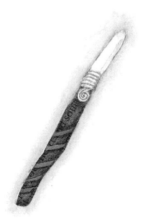

Basil and Mint Money Bags

Rather than chasing money or possessions, you can simply draw them toward you with wisdom from days gone by. Fill a tiny green pouch with the herbs basil and mint, three cinnamon sticks, one silver dollar (or a shiny pound coin), and a green stone—peridot or a smooth, mossy-colored pebble of jade would be perfect. The untrained eye might perceive this as a bag of weeds and rocks but any kitchen witch recognizes this is a powerful tool for creating dynamic change in your life and attracting good fortune.

Prepare your attraction pouch during a waxing moon; the strongest power would be when the sun or moon are in Taurus, Cancer, or Capricorn. Hold the pouch over frankincense incense and, as the smoke blesses the bag, you speak:

The moon is a silver coin; this I know.
I carry lunar magic with me everywhere I go.
Blessings upon thee and me as my abundance grows.

✳
BASIL BOUNTY

This sweet-tasting herb is excellent in savory dishes.
Basil truly grows like a weed and you should cultivate it
right on the kitchen windowsill so you can snip and add to
your Italian-inspired dishes. Give your basil plants plenty of
sun, lots of water, and you will reap a mighty bounty to share
with the neighbors. Old wives and hedge witches claim that
basil protects your home while it also brings prosperity and
happiness. Basil helps steady the mind, brings love, peace,
and money, and protects against insanity—what more can
you want? Basil has many practical magical applications
such as making peace after disagreements. The benefits of
this plant are as plentiful as the plant itself; it can be used in
attracting and getting love and, on the highest vibrational
level, abetting psychic abilities, even astral projection.

Carry this power pouch with you as you go about your day—to
work, to the store, on your daily walks, to social events. Soon,
blessings will shower down upon you. You might even receive
a gift or literally find money in your path.

Lucky Seven Almond Attraction Spell

In your pantry, you have much that you need to attract whatever you want more of into your life—love, money, a new home, a new job, increased creativity. The jar of almonds on your shelf is filled with sheer potential, and not just for delicious snacks or dessert. If you are fortunate enough to have an almond tree, harvest your own, but store-bought almonds are just as good. The great psychic Edgar Cayce ate five almonds a day for cancer prevention and believed this healthy nut contained great power. Almond oil is excellent for your skin, applied lightly as a self-blessing. A dab of almond-attraction oil will go far for you, too, in this easy and effective spell.

If you are feeling a financial pinch, try rubbing a dab of almond oil on your wallet and visualize it filling up with money. To engender greater and long-lasting change, perform this spell.

Take seven green votive candles, seven almonds, and seven flat, green leaves from a plant in your garden—ivy or geranium are excellent choices. On your kitchen table, arrange the candles in a circle, placing them on the leaves. Anoint each candle with a dab of almond oil, which works swiftly as it is ruled by Mercury, the god of speed, swift change, and fast communication who operates in the element of Air. Place the almonds in the center. At 7 a.m. or 7 p.m. for seven days, light a candle and eat one almond. Then incant aloud the following words:

Luck be quick, luck be kind.
And by lucky seven, good fortune will be mine.
As above, so below,
The wisdom of the gods shall freely flow.
To perfect possibility, in gratitude I go.

Each day, as the clock strikes seven, perform your ritual. Later, you can count your blessings; there will be at least seven!

Very Berry Enchantment Ink

⅛ cup (40ml) crushed berry juice

9 drops of burgundy wine

Dark red ink

Small metal bowl

Apple essential oil

Vial or small, sealable bottle

Paper and envelope

Feather

Red candle

In the days of yore, people often made their own inks, thus imbuing them with a deeply personal energy. They simply went to the side of the road and gathered blackberries from the vines that grew there. Often, a bird flying overhead will supply a gift of volunteer vines, best cultivated by a fence where it can climb, making berry picking easier. When it comes to matters of the heart, contracts, legal letters, and any document of real importance that you feel the need to make your mark upon, an artfully made ink can help you do just that; it can also help you write sweet love letters and memorable memorandums. This spell is best performed during the waning moon.

Mix the juice, wine, and red ink in a small, metal bowl. Carefully pour it into the vial and add one drop of the apple essence. Seal the bottle and shake gently.

Incant aloud the spell below:

> *By my hand, this spell is wrought.*
> *With this ink, I will author my own destiny.*
> *And have the happy life and love I sought.*
> *So mote it be.*

Then write the fate you envision for yourself in the near and far future, using the enchantment ink and a feather for a pen. Let it dry, seal it in an envelope and keep on your altar until the new moon phase. Then, by the light of a red candle, open the letter to yourself and read it aloud. Afterward, burn the paper using the candle, scatter the ashes in your garden and by the next new moon, you will begin to reap the positive plans you invoked.

Rainwater Renewal Spell

I advise any witchy gardener to have a rain barrel to make the most of stormy weather; you can water your garden and pots of herbs during dry and sunnier spells. On the first day of the rainfall, place a blue glass bowl outside as a water-catcher. Once filled with enough rainwater, bring it inside and place on your altar beside a lit candle. Speak these words:

Water of life, gift from the sky,
We bathe in newfound energy, making spirits fly!

Dip your fingers in the water and touch your forehead. Meditate upon the healing work you and your garden can do, thanks to the nurturing rainfall. Pour the water into the ground of your garden, speaking the spell one last time.

GARDEN YOUR WAY TO HAPPINESS

For dispelling negative energy, plant heather, hawthorn, holly, hyacinth, hyssop, ivy, juniper, periwinkle, and nasturtiums.

For healing, plant sage, wort, sorrel, carnation, onion, garlic, peppermint, and rosemary.

Farming and working with plants is guided by the moon and should take place during the waxing moon in the signs of Cancer, Scorpio, Pisces, Capricorn, and Taurus.

Coming Full Circle

"The very act of gardening will be healing. As you continue to practice kitchen witchery, you learn what works in your spells and which herbs, teas, and plant-based potions and recipes cause you and your loved ones to flourish."

cooking up love

Magic not only influences desired outcomes, but is empowering and also fosters personal growth. The carefully crafted love spells and rites of romance in this chapter cover every aspect of amour. You will learn spells that create the potential for love, draw the attention and devotion of a suitor, strengthen the union between a couple, invoke passion, and perhaps—most importantly—fill your own heart with love and compassion. The romantic repasts and aphrodisiacs are secret recipes shared here for the first time so that you can enjoy them with the one you love. Your affections will be returned threefold with the treasury of charms in this compendium.

Light of Love: Altar Dedication

Bring love into your life with this altar dedication. Use a small table or chest in your bedroom and cover it with a rich, red scarf or cloth. Adorn it with objects that signify love—red candles, ruby-colored bowls, roses, a statue of Adonis, a heart-shaped chunk of amethyst, whatever may stir your feelings and senses. Give the area a good smudging to purify the space to refresh it for new beginnings. Anoint your candles with oil of jasmine, rose, or any scent that is redolent of romance to you and prepare some similar incense. Light both and speak aloud:

> *I light the flame,*
> *I fan the flame.*
> *Each candle I burn is a wish,*
> *I desire and will be desired in return.*

Twin-Hearts Candle Consecration

If you are seeking a soul mate, this simple spell will do the trick. At nearly any new-age bookshop, you can find heart-shaped, semiprecious stones. On the next new moon, take two pieces of rose quartz and stand in the center of your bedroom. Light two pink candles and recite these words:

> *Beautiful crystal I hold this night,*
> *Flame with love for my delight.*
> *Harm to none as love comes to me.*
> *This I ask and so shall it be.*

Keep the candles and crystals on your bedside table and think of it as a shrine to love. Repeat three nights in a row and ready yourself for amour.

Mists of Avalon Potion

3 drops rose oil

3 drops lavender oil

3 drops neroli (orange blossom) essence

½ cup (120ml) pure distilled water

If you are dreaming of real romance, you can bring about visions of your future true love with this potent potion.

Pour all the ingredients into a colored-glass spray bottle and shake well three times. Fifteen minutes before you retire, spray lightly on your linens, towel, and pillowcase. Keep a dream journal on your nightstand so you can record details of the great love that will soon manifest.

Flower Charm

To light the flower of love in your heart, time this charm with the waning of a new Moon. Place a green candle beside a white lily, rose, or freesia. Make sure it is a posy of personal preference. White flowers have the greatest perfume, and any one of these beauties will impart your home with a pleasing aura. I like to float a gardenia in a clear bowl of fresh water, truly the essence of the divine. Light the candle and hold the flower close to your heart. Pray using the spell below.

Steer me to the highest light;
Guide me to beauty and truth.
Much have I to give. Much have I to live.
Bright blessings to one and all.

The Art of Spellbinding: Knotted Heartstrings

On a small piece of paper, write the name of the person whose affection you seek in red ink, then roll into a scroll. Anoint the paper with rose oil. Tie the scroll with red thread, speaking one line of the spell below per knot.

> *One knot to seek my love, one to find my love.*
> *One to bring my love, one to bind my love.*
> *Forever bound together as one.*
> *So mote it be; this charm is done.*

Keep the scroll on your love altar and burn red candles anointed with rose oil each evening until your will is done. Be very sure of your heart's desire as this spell is everlasting.

Gypsy Love Herbs

Many a gypsy woman has enjoyed the fruits of long-lasting love by reciting the following charm while mixing rye and pimento into a dish shared with the object of her affection. While stirring in these amorous herbs, declaim:

> *Rye of earth, pimento of fire,*
> *Eaten surely lights desire.*
> *Serve to he whose love I crave,*
> *And his heart I will enslave!*

✳

GROW A GARDEN OF EARTHLY DELIGHTS

A happy relationship can be cultivated, literally. By planting and carefully tending plants that have special properties—night blooming jasmine for heightened sensuality and scent, lilies for lasting commitment, roses for romance—you can nurture your marriage or partnership. During a new moon in the Venus-ruled signs of Taurus or Libra, plant an array of flowers that will enhance mutual devotion.

Flirty Friday Date-Night Magic

1 cup (240ml) sesame oil

5 drops orange blossom oil

3 drops rose oil

3 drops amber oil

The touch of Venus makes this the most festive day of the week. This is also the optimal evening for a tryst! To prepare yourself for a romantic and flirtatious Friday night, you must take a goddess bath with the following potion, stored in a special and beautiful bottle or bowl.

Combine the oils and stir with your fingers six times, silently repeating three times:

I am a daughter of Venus;
I embody love.

My body is a temple of pleasure;
I am all that is beautiful.

Tonight, I will drink fully from
the cup of love.

Pour two-thirds of this potion into a steaming bath and meditate upon your evening plans. As you finish, repeat the Venus spell once more.

Don't use a towel but allow your skin to dry naturally. Dress up in your finest goddess garb. Dab a bit of the Venusian oil mix on your pulse points, your wrists, ankles, and the base of your throat. When you are out and about this evening, you will most certainly meet lovely and stimulating new people who are very interested in you. In fact, they are being drawn to you.

Belles Lettres: RSVP for Romance

Love letters are a very old art that deepen intimacy. What heart doesn't surge when the object of affection pours passion onto a page? Magic ink, prepared paper, and wax are certain to seal the deal. Take a special sheet of paper—sumptuous handmade paper or creamy watermarked fine stationery is ideal—and write with enchanted ink, such as wine-dark dragonsblood, easily found at any metaphysical shop. You can also try the Very Berry recipe in Chapter 5 (see page 96). Perfume the letter with the signature scent or oil your lover prefers, such as amber, vanilla, or ylang-ylang. Seal the letter with a wax, which you have also scented with one precious drop of this oil and, of course, a kiss.

Before your love letter is delivered, light a candle anointed with this oil of love and intone this spell:

Eros, speed my message on wings of desire.

Make my sweetheart burn with love's pure fire.

So mote it be.

Be ready for an ardent answer!

Lover's Tea

Here is a quick recipe to create exactly the right mood for a dreamy evening.

Stir all the ingredients together in a clockwise motion. You can store this in a tin or colored jar for up to a year for those special evenings. When you are ready to brew the tea, pour boiling water over the herbs, two teaspoons for a cup of water. Say the following spell aloud during the 5-minute steeping and picture your heart's desire.

1 ounce (28g) dried hibiscus flowers

1 ounce (28g) dried and pulverized rosehips

½ ounce (14g) peppermint

½ ounce (14g) dried lemon balm

Herbal brew of love's emotion
With my wish I fortify
When two people share this potion
This love shall intensify
As in the Olde Garden of Love.

Sweeten to taste with honey and share this luscious libation with the one you love most of all.

Aphrodite's Ageless Skin Potion

¼ cup (60ml) sweet almond oil (as a base)

2 drops chamomile oil

2 drops rosemary oil

2 drops lavender oil

You will notice that many a witch appears ageless. There is a good reason for this; we manifest a lot of joy in our life, including creating potions to take excellent care of our skin for Aphrodite-like youthfulness.

Combine these oils in a sealable, dark-blue bottle. Shake very thoroughly and prepare to anoint your skin with this invocation:

Goddess of Love, Goddess of Light, hear this prayer,
Your youth, beauty, and radiance, please share.
So mote it be.

Clean your skin with warm water, then gently daub with the potion. You can also make a salve or balm using my recipe if you want to turn the clock backward. Prepare to be asked for your beauty secrets.

Anointed Lips

From time immemorial, witches have enchanted with their magical beauty. That is because we know how to supplement Mother Nature's gifts. Before a special evening, employ a "kiss of glamour" by adding one drop of clove oil to your favorite pot of lip gloss. While stirring gently, say the following words aloud three times.

The ripest fruit,
The perfect petal,
Each kiss is a spell of utmost bliss.
And so it is.

This will make your lips tingle in a delightful way and give your kisses a touch of spice. The lucky recipient of your affection will be spellbound.

Coming Full Circle

"At the end of life, all that matters is how much love you gave to the world, how much of your heart you shared with people."

celebrating the wheel of the year

The pagan calendar reminds us of the cycles of nature and the importance of spending time in community. Nearly all our modern high holidays have ancient roots in farming customs and fertility rituals to ensure good crops and plenty for all. Lunar moon festivals, solstice seasonal galas, and major sabbat celebrations call for ceremonial magic, family feasts, and acknowledgment of the natural world. Observing these high holy days with the circle rites, magical foods, and pagan prayers herein assures that your kitchen will be a temple dedicated to joy for many years to come.

Mystical Meals and Holiday Rituals

Sabbats are the holy days for each season of the year, in accordance with the celestial spheres above. Some of these holy days celebrate the arrival of spring and the start of new growth, while others mark the harvest in preparation for the dark and chilly days of winter. Nearly all our festivals have roots in the ancient rites based in fertility and the hopes of abundant farm crops. Humankind first marked time by the movement of the stars, Sun, and Moon in the sky, which also informed the designation of constellations and astrological calendars. Candlemas, Beltane, Lammas Day, and All Hallow's Eve are the major sabbats. The lesser sabbats, listed below, are the astrological markers of new seasons:

* Ostara: March 21, also known as the Vernal or Spring Equinox

* Litha: June 21, commonly known as the Summer Solstice

* Mabon: September 21, best known as the Autumnal Equinox

* Yule: December 21, is the Winter Solstice

Cakes and Ale: Saturn-Day Night Fever

Here is a pagan party plan, which is wonderful for weekend evenings. You can add many embellishments, such as important astrological or lunar happenings, but you should gather your friends or coven and celebrate life any Saturday night of your choosing. If the weather is warm enough, have the festivities outside. Otherwise, make sure to choose an indoor space with enough room for dancing, drumming, and major merriment. Ask each of your guests to bring cake, cookies, and candies of their choice along with their favorite beer, wine, mead, cider, or ale, and sitting cushions. Place the offerings on a center-table altar and light candles of all colors. Once everyone is seated and settled, the host or designated circle leader chants:

> *Gods of Nature, bless these cakes,*
> *That we may never suffer hunger.*
> *Goddess of the harvest, bless this ale,*
> *That we may never suffer thirst.*
> *Blessed be.*

The eldest and the youngest should serve the food and drink to all in the circle. Lastly, they serve each other and the leader chants the blessing again. Let the feasting begin!

Candlemas: The Joyful Coming Season

Candlemas, on February 2, also known as Imbolc, is the highest point between the winter solstice and spring equinox. This festival anticipates the coming of spring with banquets and blessings. Tradition holds that milk must be served and modern pagans have expanded that to butter cookies, ice cream, and

cheeses; and any other related food should be shared. It is an important time to welcome new members of your spiritual circle and new witches into a coven. Candlemas is a heartwarming occasion, but it is still a wintry time so kindling for the hearth or bonfire should include cedar, pine, juniper, and holly along with wreaths of the same to mark the four cardinal points, alongside white candles in glass votives. Strong incense such as cedar, nag champa, or frankincense will bless the space. The circle leader shall begin the ritual by lighting incense from the fire, facing each direction, and saying:

Welcome Guardians of the East, bringing your fresh winds and breath of life. Come to the circle of Imbolc.

Welcome Guardians of the South, you bring us heart and health. Come to the circle on this holy day.

Welcome Guardians of the West, place of setting sun and mighty mountains. Come to us.

Welcome Guardians of the North, land of life-giving rains and snow. Come to our circle on this sacred day.

The leader should welcome each member of the circle and speak of the gifts they bring to the community. Everyone should acknowledge one another with toasts and blessings and break bread together in this time of the coming season.

Spiritual Spring Cleaning: the Bean Blessing

The change of season at the Vernal Equinox, on March 21, brings about the need for new energies, which you can engender with cleansing. Here is an ancient way to cast out "the old" and bring in glad tidings and positive new beginnings for your circle of friends and family.

Grab a bag of beans from your kitchen and invite your circle over. In ancient times, many pagan peoples, from Incans to Egyptians and Greeks, believed beans contained evil spirits, so this rite comes from that lineage. Go to your roof or the highest point of your house which you can get to safely and give everyone a handful of beans. Each person throws one bean at a time, calling out whatever they need to bid goodbye to—a bad habit, nightmare job, damaged relationship, whatever your personal demons may be. After everyone has tossed the negativity and discord away, celebrate the clean slate. Fun note, if you toss lentils into a barren field in the spring, by fall, you will be able to harvest enough for many pots of soup!

✳
SPROUT INTO SPRING ALL YEAR-ROUND

Sprouts are immensely nutritious and fairly effortless to grow:
add one teaspoon of seeds to a quart jar filled with water
and cover with cheesecloth. After 24 hours, turn the jar
upside down and drain. After at least 2 hours, refill and
repeat this process twice a day for 3–5 days. You'll have a
rich repast for salads, sandwiches, soups, and stir fries.
Try these other seeds for endless healthy options: sunflower,
mung bean, broccoli, quinoa, lentil, radish, mustard, alfalfa,
red clover, and fenugreek.

Beltane Eve

Beltane, celebrated on April 30, is without doubt the sexiest of pagan high holidays, and it is anticipated greatly throughout the year. Witchy ones celebrate this holy night, and it is traditional for celebrations to last all through the night. This is a festival for feasting, singing, laughter, and lovemaking. On May Day, when the sun returns in the morning, revelers gather to erect a merrily beribboned Maypole to dance around, followed by picnics and sensual siestas. The recipe opposite is befitting this special time of the year when love flows as freely as wine.

Beltane Brew

Honeyed mead is revered as the drink of choice for this sexiest of pagan holy days. It is an aphrodisiac and signals the ripeness of this day devoted to love and lust. This recipe is adapted from a medieval method.

Mix the honey and water. Boil for 5 minutes. You can add the herbs to your liking but I prefer a tablespoon each of clove, nutmeg, cinnamon, and allspice. Add a packet of yeast and then mix. Put everything in a large container. Cover with plastic wrap and allow to rise and expand. Store the mix in a dark place and allow it to set for seven days, ideally at the beginning of a new-moon phase. Refrigerate for three days while the sediment settles at the bottom. Strain and store in a colored glass bottle, preferably green. You can drink it now but after seven months, it will have gained a full-bodied flavor. Always keep in a cool dark place.

1 quart (1 liter) honey

3 quarts (3 liters) distilled water

Herbs to flavor, such as cinnamon, nutmeg, or vanilla, according to your preference

1 packet (7g) of active dry yeast

Nonalcoholic Mead

1 quart (1 liter) honey

3 quarts (3 liters) distilled water

½ cup (120ml) lemon juice

1 lemon, sliced

½ teaspoon nutmeg

pinch of salt

Boil all the mixed ingredients for five minutes and let cool. You will need to bottle this immediately in a colored glass jar. Keep this in the fridge to avoid fermentation and enjoy during any festive occasion. This is a healthy and refreshing way to celebrate.

Hoof and Horn Rite

Ideally, you would celebrate outdoors, but if indoor-bound on Beltane Eve, pick a place with a fireplace and have a roaring blaze, so celebrants can wear comfy clothing and dance barefoot. Ask them to bring spring flowers and musical instruments, plenty

of drums! Place pillows on the floor and serve an ambrosial spread of finger foods, honeyed mead, beer, spiced cider, wine, and fruity teas. As you light circle incense, set out green, red, and white candles, one for each participant. When it is time to call the circle, raise your arm and point to each direction, saying "To the east, to the north," etc., then sing:

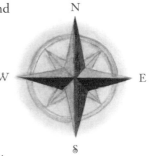

Hoof and horn, hoof and horn, tonight our spirits are reborn [repeat thrice]

Welcome, joy, to this home. Fill these friends with love and laughter.

So mote it be.

Have each guest light a candle and speak to the subject of love with a toast of Beltane Brew. Drumming and dancing is the next part of the circle. This is truly an invocation of lust for life and will be a night to remember for all. Now rejoice!

Sacred Grove Solstice Spell

Celebrating the season of the sun, on June 21, is best done outdoors in the glory of nature's full bloom. If you have a forest nearby or a favorite grove of trees, plan to picnic and share this rite of passage with your spiritual circle. Covens often have a favorite spot. All the better if a great oak is growing there, the tree most sacred to druids. Gather the tribe and bring brightly colored ribbons and indelible markers. Form the circle by holding hands, then point to east, south, north, and west, chanting:

> *We hold the wisdom of the sun,*
> *We see the beauty of our earth.*
> *To the universe that gives us life, we return the gift.*
> *Deepest peace to all,*
> *And we are all one. Blessed be.*

Each member of the circle should speak their wish for the world, themselves, or loved ones and write it on a ribbon. One by one, tie your ribbon to a tree. Each flutter of the wind will spread your well wishes.

Summer Solstice Pudding

Inspired by a traditional recipe from Kent, known affectionately as "The Garden of England," this summer pudding brings forth the taste of the season, simply sublime.

    Combine all the fruit and sugar in a saucepan and gently boil for 3 minutes. Squeeze in the juice of half a lemon. Line a big bowl with the bread, overlapping to form a crust. Pour in the fruit mix. Add one last bread slice to cover the mixture and place a saucer on top with a weight on it to press down. Cover with plastic wrap and chill in the refrigerator overnight. Before serving, turn the dish upside down and the pudding will slip out in a half-circle shape. Top with fresh whipped cream and a few berries and mint leaves as garnish. This cool treat could not be easier, and each spoonful is filled with the sweetness of summer.

1 pound (450g) fresh mixed berries—strawberries, raspberries, blueberries, blackberries

1 cup (225g) diced fresh peaches, plums, nectarines

¼ cup (50g) sugar

juice of ½ lemon

10 slices crust-less bread (or 15 biscuits or shortbreads)

Lammas Day: Harvesting Happiness

This major sabbat, on August 2, denotes the high point of the year; the crops are in their fullness, the weather is warm, and the countryside is bursting forth with the beauty of life. Pagans know we have the heavens above to thank for this and the gods of nature must be acknowledged for their generosity with a gathering of the tribe and a feast, ideally in the great outdoors.

Ask invitees to bring harvest-themed offerings for the altar: gourds, pumpkins, bundles of wheat stalks and corn, fresh pickings from their garden, and thanksgiving themed food to share—pies, tomato salads, cucumber pickles, green beans, corn pudding, watermelon, lemon cakes, apple cider, and beer brewed from wheat, hops, and barley. This celebration of the harvests of the summer season should reflect what you have grown with your own hands. Fill your cauldron or a big, beautiful colored glass bowl half-full with freshly drawn water and get packets of tiny votive candles to float in it.

At the feast table, make sure to have a place setting for the godly guest Lugh, who watched over the plantings to ensure this bounty. Place loaves of Lammas bread by his plate.

When all guests have arrived, everyone should add a food offering to the plate of the god and light a candle to float in the cauldron. Cut a slice of Lammas bread for Lugh and begin the ceremony with this prayer of thanks:

Oh, ancient Lugh of the fields and farms,
We invite you here with open arms,
In this place between worlds, in flowering fields of hay.
You have brought the blessings we receive this Lammas Day.

Begin the feast and, before the dessert course, everyone should go around the table and speak of their gratitude for the gifts of the year. Storytelling, singing, spiral dances, and all manner of merriment are part of Lammas Day.

Lugh Lore: Guardian of the Harvest

The "Shining One" from the Celtic mythology, Lugh is the warrior sun god and also guardian of crops. The Lughnassa festival honors the harvest god, taking place at the beginning of every August. Lammas, which means "loaf mass," was the Anglo Saxon's fete for the first harvest of the year and included sport competitions in addition to feasting, dancing, and ritual.

The Scottish caber toss, a log-throwing contest, derives from this sort of yearly folk Olympics. These two early-August festivals were conflated over the centuries, with Lammas becoming ingrained in the pagan calendar.

At the end of summer and fall, kitchen witches should hold rituals of gratitude for the abundance of the crops and for the gift that is life. This will keep the flow of prosperity coming to you and yours. Lugh also has domain over late-summer storms, so anyone experiencing drought or wildfires can pray to Lugh for rains to come.

Lammas Day Bread

This recipe can make 1 large or 2 regular loaves.

Mix the dry ingredients in a large bowl. Add the peanut butter and honey to the hot milk and stir to combine. Cool the milk mixture to warm and pour into the dry ingredients. Knead for 15 minutes, adding the extra flour, if needed, to make a smooth and elastic dough. Oil the surface of the dough, cover with plastic wrap or a damp kitchen towel, and let rise in a warm place until it has doubled in size; this usually takes 90 minutes. Punch it down and shape into your desired loaf size. Allow to rise again, covered in a warm place.

Bake in a preheated oven at 375°F/190°C/gas mark 5 for 30 minutes until golden brown and hollow-sounding when you rap on the bottom.

2 cups (270g) whole-wheat flour, plus an additional ½ cup (70g) set aside

2 cups (270g) bread flour

¼ cup (35g) toasted sesame seeds

2 tablespoons active dry yeast

2½ teaspoons salt

2 tablespoons peanut butter

2 tablespoons honey

2 cups (475ml) milk, scalded

Fall Equinox Festival: Mabon

Your kitchen is not just where you prepare meals, concoct healing tonics, and craft enchantments; it is also a temple with an altar where you honor spirit. This change-of-seasons sabbat of Mabon, on September 21, marks the turning of weather and the other face of nature. Mark the four directions on your altar with a loaf of bread in the east, a bowl of apples in the south, a bottle of wine in west, and an ear of Indian corn in the north.

LEAFY LEGEND—GRABBING LUCK BY THE HAND

Here is a sweet bit of alchemy available to all, handed down
from medieval times. Wise women of yore taught their
children to look for falling leaves. To catch one in your hand
is the best kind of luck, directly from Mother Nature herself.
Carry it with you for a season and you will be safe from harm
and find gifts in your path. If you are especially blessed to
catch two leaves in one season, the second is for your
companion of destiny. You will be bound by both feeling
and fortune.

Samhain: All Hallows' Eve

Halloween, on October 31, stems from the grand tradition of the Celtic New Year. What started as a folk festival celebrated by small groups in rural areas has come to be the second largest holiday nowadays in North America and is increasingly gaining popularity in the UK and the rest of Europe. This holiday satisfies a basic human need to let your "wild side" out, and connect with the ancient ways. This is the time when the veil between worlds is thinnest and you can commune with the other side, with elders, and the spirit world. It is important to honor the ancestors during this major sabbat and acknowledge what transpired in the passing year and set intentions for the coming one.

This is the ideal time to invite your circle; the ideal number for your "coven" is 13. Gather powdered incense, salt, a loaf of bread, goblets for wine, and three candles to represent the triple goddess for altar offerings. Ideally on an outdoor stone altar, pour the powdered incense into a pentagram star shape. Let go of old sorrows, angers, and anything not befitting new beginnings in this new year. Bring only your best to this auspicious occasion.

Light the candles and say:

> *In honor of the Triple Goddess on this sacred night*
> *of Samhain,*
>
> *All the ancient ones,*
>
> *From time before time,*
>
> *To those behind the veil.*

Rap the altar three times and light the incense. Say this blessing:

For this bread, wine, and salt,
We ask the blessings of Mother, Maiden, and Crone,
And the gods who guard the Gate of the World.

Sprinkle salt over the bread, eat the bread, and drink the wine.

Each of the celebrants should come to the altar repeating the bread and wine blessing. After this, be seated and everyone in turn should name those on the other side and offer thanks to ancestors and deities. This can and should take a long time as we owe much to loved ones on the other side.

New Year's Kitchen

A form of magic handed down from antiquity is to have a figure of a domestic goddess in your home; archaeologists have found them amongst the most ancient artifacts. It is a good energy generator to have such a figurine decorating your kitchen altar. The most important consideration is to choose the divinity with which you feel the deepest connection.

Global Goddesses Every Kitchen Witch Should Know

* Chicomecoatl: this Aztec corn goddess bring prosperity to farmers

* Dugnai: this Slavic deity is a house guardian and blesser of breads

* Fornax: here is the goddess of all ovens, Roman in origin; she guards against hunger

* Frigg: this benevolent Nordic being watches over the domestic arts (including love)

* Fuchi: the Japanese invoke her when they need fires— cooking fire, campfire, and celebrations

* Hebe: daughter of Hera and Zeus, this goddess of youth is also a cupbearer who can bless your chalices and kitchen ritual vessels

* Hehsui-no-kami: in Japan, she is the kitchen goddess and she can be yours, too

* Huixtocihuatl: the Aztec goddess of salt is one to turn to and thank each and every day

* Ida: the subcontinent of India looks to her who rules fire and spiritual devotion

* Ivenopae: the Indonesian mother of rice helps at harvest time, feeding millions

* Li: nourishing fires is the charge of this Chinese goddess

* Nikkai: the first fruits of the season are the gifts of this Canaanite holiness

* Ogetsu-hime: this dependable deity is the Japanese goddess of food

* Okitsu-hime: revered from ancient times is this Japanese kitchen goddess

* Pirua: Peru's mother of maize is sacred to all who rely on her for survival

* Pomona: the fruit goddess of Roman times has domain over gardens and orchards

* Saule: this Baltic benefic is a sun goddess who lights the hearth fires along with all homely arts

Yule: Winter Solstice Bonfire

December is named for the Roman goddess Decima, one of the three fates. The word "yule" comes from the Old Norse *jol*, which means midwinter and is celebrated on the shortest day of the year, December 21. The tradition was to have a vigil at a bonfire to make sure the sun did indeed rise again. This primeval custom evolved to become a storytelling evening and while it may well be too cold to sit outside in snow and sleet, sitting or congregating around a blazing hearthfire, dining, and talking deep into the night are still important for your community truly to know one another, impart wisdom, and speak of hopes and dreams. Greet the new sun with stronger connections and a shared vision for the coming solar year.

✳
WINTER-IS-COMING ROOT ROAST

We live in a time when some of the very foods the early Yule celebrants feasted upon are having a renaissance—bone broths, root vegetables, and stone fruits. These are simple to prepare and share with the clan. The following root veggies are magnificent when roasted with rosemary for 40 minutes at 450°F/230°C/gas mark 8 with a drizzling of olive oil and salt: 2 pounds (1kg) mix-and-match medium-sized yams, potatoes, garlic, mushrooms, onions, parsnips, carrots, and beets. In the rare chance of leftovers, these can become the basis for a heart-warming soup or stew.

Coming Full Circle

"This path is not only about looking inward, but also about becoming attuned to the world around you—every leaf, stone, blade, flower, and seed; the highest calling of any pagan is to achieve harmony with the cycles of the natural world."

conclusion:

Journaling Your Spellcraft

The art and practice of kitchen witchery is, at the core, an expression of your spirituality. While many of the sabbat celebrations and circle rites are gatherings of the tribe, much of your spellcraft will be performed by a coven of one—you. And it is the "inner work" of devising and creating personal rituals, tracking life cycles of the moon and stars, and recording your magical workings in your Book of Shadows that will best encourage your deepest spiritual development. Your life is a work in progress and here is a record of it. The insights you gain from going back and considering all that has come before are priceless.

These next few pages of prompts are
all for you to record your magical musings
and inspired ideas in your own journal. Keep these
and look back now and again for reflection. You may
discover that the prompts included here were the first
steps in renewal and new directions set in your life.
This record of your wisdom is a priceless treasure.

Blessed be from my kitchen to yours!

* The new-Moon phase is the time
for fresh ventures, renewing, cleansing,
and clearing. What seeds will you sow
during this time for new beginnings?

* A waxing moon is the time for abundance,
attraction, and love magic. It can also heal rifts and
protect existing relationships. What do you want to
attract during this time?

* The full Moon shines a light on challenges in your life; now is the time to release and let go of anything causing problems. What are the issues or old patterns you should "catch and release"?

* The waning moon is a time to emphasize the positive by banishing the negative. Rid yourself of any unconstructive feelings, habits, health challenges, or thoughts; clear out the psychic clutter with the spells you have learned and replace it with good energy. What psychic clutter do you need to clear?

* Circles and group rituals often occur only on high holy days. What is some of the solo spellwork you want to explore during the rest of the year? What rituals would you like to design and create?

* Intention-setting is one of the most powerful ways through which you can bring positive change into your life. It is a vital kind of inner-work. What are your magical intentions and visions for the days and weeks to come?

* As your garden grows, so does your wisdom and well-being. Which plants, potions, herbs, and flowers function best in your magical workings? Which would you like to add for the next spring?

* Your home is your sanctuary. As a kitchen witch and practitioner of house magic, how can you create a more peaceful, beautiful, healthy, and happy domicile for yourself and your loved ones?

Acknowledgments

I have much to be thankful for in my life and I count among my blessings the CICO "Dream Team." I have been writing and publishing for several years and I have never experienced such a plentitude of grace and good work. Kudos to publisher Cindy Richards for this exemplar in the world of book publishing. I am grateful to in-house editor Carmel Edmonds for polishing this book into a jewel and for Jennifer Jahn's eagle-eyed copyediting. Emma Garner's luscious illustrations are simply delightful and, along with Emily Breen's expert design, they bring the pages to life. Heaps of gratitude to the one-and-only Kristine Pidkameny who guided this project from idea to reality and made it fun in the process. I am inspired by all of you!